BEGINNERS
PRACTICE MANUAL

ORIT SEN-GUPTA

VIJNANA BOOKS

First edition, printed May 2009
Second edition, printed November 2012

VIJNANA BOOKS
WWW.VIJNANAYOGA.ORG
ORIT.SEN@GMAIL.COM

CONTENTS

A. Introduction

B. Daily Practice

A. Introduction

Vijnana Yoga
Practicing, feeling, understanding - from inside

Sources for the term Vijnana:

> **Vijñāna** - *the act of distinguishing or discerning, understanding, recognizing; intelligence, knowledge, skill, art, science*
> (Monier Williams Sanskrit-English Dictionary)

"Verily, different from and within the sheath consisting of mind (manas) is the atma consisting of vijnana (understanding). This has the form of a person...
> Faith (śraddhā) is its head,
> Order (ṛta) is its right side.
> Truth (satya) is its left side.
> Yoga is its body.
> The Great Intelligence (mahat) is its lower part, the foundation."
> (Taittirīya Upaniṣad II.4.1)

"At the stage of mind (manas), we accept authority which is external.
At the stage of vijnana, internal growth is affected. We develop faith, order, truthfulness and union with the supreme."
> (from S. Radhakrishnan's commentary on the Taittirīya Upaniṣad)

Beginning a Daily Practice

Many years ago I learned from Dona Holleman the 'Full Program' outlined in the Vijnana Yoga Practice Manual. Dona told me that this was the teaching she received from Mr. B.K.S. Iyengar when she studied and practiced with him in the sixties. Some years ago while reprinting this full program we added an intermediate program to answer the needs of many students who were overwhelmed by the length and density of the full program. Since then I have been asked - and what about beginners?

I am happy now to introduce the Vijnana Yoga Practice Manual for Beginners. This is a simple manual; the drawings of the poses are taken from the 'little' yoga book and placed in an easy format you can lay next to your mat.

Create a special space and time where you can practice, and a calm and clean place where you are unlikely to be disturbed. Early mornings or evenings are good times for practice. If possible practice regularly in the same place and at the same time. In any case it is always good to begin each day with a short session of sitting and prāṇāyāma in order to connect with yourself before going out into the world.

Whenever you begin āsana practice, feel your body from inside. If you are stiff, gently warm up with mild leg stretches and twists while lying on your back.

Afterwards begin āsana practice with a few sun salutations and standing poses. You can then add a short sequence of forward bends, hand balances, backbends or sitting positions. Finish the practice with leg stretches and the inverted poses if you are practicing them. Finally, make sure you take the time to lie down for śavāsana (relaxation).

Make an effort not to push yourself or strive for success. If you can maintain a concentrated yet gentle practice continually over a long period of time, you will enjoy the practice, avoid unnecessary injuries, and find that your body and mind are changing spontaneously and effortlessly. Slowly, with the guidance of your teacher and from listening and practicing from inside, you will evolve and develop in yoga. Try to practice at least five days a week, even if you have only 20 minutes a day. Continuity in practice brings about knowledge of one's self and heartfelt devotion.

December 2008, Jerusalem

Guidelines for Practice

Fifteen years ago I spent some time in a small mountain monastery in the Galilee. One of the Christian monks there did yoga and asked me what my daily practice was. I was embarrassed, as I had no clear answer. After 11 years of being a committed yoga student I hadn't yet been initiated into the secrets of a steady daily practice.

Intuitively I realized the great lack. The so-called freedom to choose each day what to do, the absence of clear guidelines that give direction and a framework, was more a burden than a joy.

Afterwards, when I met Dona Holleman and began to practice with her, I felt gratitude for the simplicity and the clarity of a defined daily practice. There was wholeness to each of the practices, and a weekly framework that held them together in a proper balance. It was for me the perfect outlet and means to express the yearning of the heart.

Dona explained to me that this was how she had learned yoga from Mr. Iyengar when she first began to study with him in the sixties. Every day in the morning there was prāṇāyāma then āsana (each day a different group of āsanas) and in the afternoon Headstand and Shoulder Stand. Till today I practice as I learned from my teacher, body to body, and still find the practice stimulating and refining, a teaching in itself.

The heart of yoga is practice. When yoga is practiced correctly and continuously over an extended period of time with devotion, its secrets reveal themselves, supporting and enriching us. From the firmness of posture, to the steadiness of mind, to a refined breath, yoga uplifts us day by day in our most minute ways of being and functioning.

Over the years the way of practice as elaborated in this Practice Manual has become the practice of many. For those who have undertaken this way as well as for their students the Practice Manual has been reorganized and slightly modified. The main objective has been to clarify the daily practice itself.

When we place the Practice Manual beside the mat, we need to regard its instructions as guidelines and not rules. Many of us have benefited from the systemizing of the practice. Even so this is an 'Open Manual'. Though there are directives concerning the order of the āsanas and the days on which they are to be practiced, we need to be watchful that the outcome of this order will not be fundamentalism or rigidity.

For yoga to blossom, listening and responding to what one hears from inside is the golden rule. Within the framework created, there is space for adapting the practice to the particular needs of the day or the person. There is always place to change the order of some of the sequences or the days on which they are practiced, to practice softly or more vigorously. The poses can be done separately or in Vinyasa or with Sūrya Namaskar or in a combination of the last two. This, according to the different needs of each person, day by day.

It is important to remember that the mere repetition of the various daily practices is not enough. The quality of the practice depends on a deep listening and responding to the body, heart and mind.

The Principles are that deep listening and constant response through subtle adjustments. They are the very core of practice. Relaxing, intensifying the mind, focusing through intent, rooting, connecting, and an awareness of the breath are not ideas or tools; they are a way of being, of functioning.

Using the Practice Manual without applying the principles may lead to a technical and shallow practice at best. There can also be the more unpleasant outcome of injuries if we treat yogic practices as mere physical techniques.

Finally, yoga practice is not isolated from our everyday life. What we ate yesterday, when we went to sleep, our relationships at work and home - all these walk with us onto the mat and ask for attention and readjustment. The very fabric of our personal lives is the material for our practice. It is this fabric that meets the fire of practice and the intensity of heart.

Thus the mat becomes a place of meeting between the deep waters of our spirit - the eternal spark within us - and our persona, our life. On the way to the depths or on the way back, we are in middle waters; in these, skillfulness and presence of mind are of utmost importance. By enhancing the fire of practice to bring light to these areas of the self, by not shunning or avoiding these spaces, our practice becomes a daily attempt to connect the deep within to the whole of ourselves.

This has always been the goal of yoga: to connect the upper and lower worlds and rediscover the inherent oneness of all life.

"All Life is Yoga", says Sri Aurobindo.

May the use of this manual be a small step towards the understanding of that.

Jerusalem 2001

The Principles

1. Relaxing the Body

In the beginning, relax the body. Inhale, and with the exhalation release tension. Inhale, and with the following exhalation scan the body from top to bottom and from the bottom upwards.

Wherever there is gripping or tension - relax.

The mind is looking at the body with a parental eye. With time one can observe tense areas releasing and expanding into space. If areas of weakness are noticed, inhale into them with courage and enliven them with energy. Let excess leave the body; relax. Thus the body becomes stable and quiet.

2. Quieting the Mind

When we position ourselves on the mat we distance ourselves from our responsibility to react to the world. The eyes look inward to catch the inner mood, the state of mind.

Whether we are concentrated, dispersed or nervous; happy, sad or angry; whether we are afraid, tired or energetic - the eyes are positioned at the back of the head.

We observe ourselves and our practice from an inner silence. With each inhalation the eyes sink deeper into the back of the head. With each exhalation there is an intensification of concentration.

Empty Mind intensifies itself in practice.

3. Intent

Now the body and mind are at ease and stable, quiet and concentrated. From this place we see our objective - Sitting, Prāṇāyāma, Āsana - and direct ourselves towards it.

The mind directs itself to the practice; the body awaits the practice; the heart embraces the practice with all its might.

With each inhalation there is an intensification of intent, with each exhalation the sharpening of its direction. By visualizing ourselves sitting, breathing, moving, or by imagining another person in that practice we devote ourselves wholly to it. With each breath, with each pose we reaffirm our intent.

4. Rooting

The mind rests at the place where the body touches the earth. Let the weight of the body sink into this place - for example, the feet. Intensify the weight pressing down, as if the foot would like to sink into the earth, and then feel the power of that downward movement flowing through the body. As the roots of a tree deepen and widen into the earth, so the branches above expand into the sky.

It is easy to understand the idea behind rooting, yet surprisingly difficult to execute it in every movement and posture. As rooting is mastered, the body becomes light and loose and moves without effort.

5. Connecting

Always be conscious of two opposite directions that are connected to each other. To go up, go down. To go forwards, shift into the back. Wishing for the left side, steady yourself on the right. Wishing to expand, come from the core.

The first direction is the arrow, the second direction is the bow; the thread that binds them is Connecting. In each pose the farthest limb from the ground connects to that which is rooting into the ground. Every single body part in between is whole in itself, a distinct, functioning unit. All the parts are balanced and work together in harmony.

Like a chain floating in space, the rings that make up the chain never touch each other. The more each part is distinct, the more the connection between them remains steady - the body in any situation moves in oneness.

6. Breathing

Be aware of inhaling, of exhaling. Inhale - go deep within; exhale - connect to the world. Inhale - accept what is; exhale - give yourself to the earth.

Inhale along the body, exhale and root. Inhale and connect the farthest parts, exhale and move into the final pose.

While inhaling the body elongates and widens, while exhaling it steadies itself in rooting and connecting. At times the breath is sweet and soft, at times it is deep and long. Sometimes the exhalation lasts longer than the inhalation, sometimes it is short and decisive.

At times only in the background, at times the source of action, breath is always present.

7. Expanding - Elongating and Widening

When there is rooting while exhaling, inhaling brings about elongation and widening. Or perhaps the elongating and widening, that occur as a result of rooting, allow for inhalation.

When elongating and widening occur, not one ring touches another as the chain called body moves in space. Then there is no sagging into the joints, no effort in the muscles. The skeleton shields its coverings, the coverings create space for the skeleton. Thus the body moves about - relaxed and connected - one.

Finally

All the principles coexist and need to be applied at all times, yet it is difficult to oversee their functions simultaneously. In order to deepen our understanding of the principles, we need to choose one that attracts us and work with it constantly until it is mastered. Many times we can work with one or two principles for a few years until these penetrate and become second nature to us.

This while remembering that it is only when all the principles coexist simultaneously in practice, that the practice is whole. Therefore when we practice yet feel 'stuck' we need to look carefully and find which principle is neglected, and then revive it.

Health Precautions

This manual is in no way meant to serve as a means for learning prāṇāyāma or āsana. It is intended that it be used in conjunction with live study, preferably with a teacher who has learned and practices by this system.

In case you are suffering from any medical problems or chronic illness, have recently had surgery, given birth, or are pregnant, it is imperative that you consult with both a yoga teacher and a physician before practicing prāṇāyāma or āsana according to this Practice Manual.

A Note on Pronunciation

The following is a partial guide to the pronunciation of Sanskrit transliteration.

Vowels:

a	like the u in hut	example: Eka Pāda
ā	like the a in father	example: Prāṇāyāma, Āsana
i	like the i in sit	example: Piṇḍāsana
ī	like the ee in sleep	example: Pīncha Mayūrāsana, Viparīta
u	like the u in put	example: Adho Mukha
ū	like the oo in hoot	example: Mūla Bandha
ṛ	like the ri in rich	example: Vṛkṣāsana, Parivṛtta
ai	like the i in smile	example: Bhairavāsana
o	like the o in home	example: Baddha Koṇāsana

Consonants:

ś and ṣ	like the sh in ship	example: Pārśva, Uṣṭrāsana, Śīrṣāsana
th	like the th in pothole	example: Jaṭhara, Haṭha Yoga
c and ch	like the ch in chair	example: Chaturanga, Citta

In general, syllables with long vowels (ā, ī, ū) are accented, receiving stress, as in Samādhi, Viparīta, Ūrdhva Dhanurāsana.

B. Daily Practice

Just Sitting - Dhyāna

The instruction is, to sit every day, in a good posture, for a regular length of time:

Sit in a comfortable position, the back effortlessly erect, the sitting bones seated on the ground, on a cushion or on a folded blanket.

If we look at the body from the side, the shoulder is above the pelvis, the ear above the shoulder, the back at ease. The spinal column is not tilted either to the left or to the right, neither forward nor backwards.

The eyes are closed gently, and can be opened at times. The gaze is turned inwards. The back of the neck is long and wide.

While sitting, we create a neutral space, in which consciousness can return to its own form.[1]

At first we may see endless feelings, emotions and thoughts; we may have to deal with fatigue, agitation, boredom and frustration. Unpleasant and pleasant memories may occur; we may discover within ourselves fears of the future.

The very watching, patiently, of whatever comes up within us - that is the practice. With time, consciousness becomes clearer, sharper, and deepens into itself. Concentration intensifies into meditation, until "that shines forth as the object only".[2]

---

1   tadā draṣṭuḥ sva-rūpe'vasthānam - "Then the dwelling of the See'er in his own form." The Yoga Sūtras of Patañjali, chapter I, sūtra 3

2   tad-eva-artha-mātra-nirbhāsaṃ sva-rūpa-śūnya-iva-samādih - "When that shines forth as the object only, as if (consciousness is) empty of its own form - Samādhi." The Yoga Sūtras of Patañjali, chapter III, sūtra 3

Kriyās and Prāṇāyāma

Kriyās and prāṇāyāma should always be practiced carefully and gently, never overstraining the lungs or nervous system. Limit yourself to no more than 15 minutes a day of these practices. The kriyās can be done all together in the early morning before or after evacuation. Prāṇāyāma is usually done in the morning before the āsanas. A short break should be taken between prāṇāyāma and āsana practice. Each of the prāṇāyāma exercises should be practiced for no more then 10 minutes at a time. Choose three prāṇāyāma exercises each morning. Remember that overly strenuous practice of prāṇāyāma may lead to irritability and over-sensitivity. Pregnant women and people with chronic medical problems should avoid the kriyās and breath-retention (kumbhaka).

Kriyās
- **Uḍḍīyāna Bandha** - 3 cycles

Prāṇāyāma
1. **Kapālabhāti**
   a. Gentle Kapālabhāti I - 1 min. cycle (Inhale 5 sec. Kapālabhāti 15 sec.inhale 10 sec. kumbhaka 20 sec. exhale 10 sec.) Repeat up to 10 times.
   b. Classical Kapālabhāti (1 minute x 3 of Kapālabhāti)

2. **Ujjāyi**
   a. Inhalation and Exhalation
   b. Inhalation, Antara Kumbhaka, Exhalation
   c. Sama-vṛtti of a. and b.

3. **Anuloma Viloma**
   a. Gradual Inhalation, Smooth Exhalation
   b. Smooth Inhalation, Gradual Exhalation

4. **Nāḍī Śodhana**
    a. Gentle Nāḍī Śodhana I (without hands)
    b. Gentle Nāḍī Śodhana II (hands on the back and chest)

v   Note: There are other prāṇāyāma practices that are not
    mentioned here.

Practice is the effort of remaining there.
But it becomes firmly grounded when done intensively,
properly and continuously over a long period.
Patañjali's Yoga Sūtra I.13-14

The āsana (pose) is stable and pleasant.
By relaxation of effort and by coming together with the infinite.
Patañjali's Yoga Sūtra II.46-47

Sūrya Namaskar - Sun Salutation

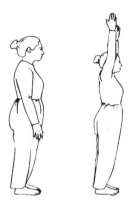

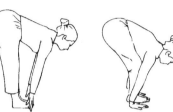

Tāḍāsana

Uttānāsana

Chaturanga

Ūrdhva Mukha Śvānāsana

Adho Mukha Śvānāsana
(Dog Pose)

Uttānāsana

Tāḍāsana

Standing Poses

Vṛkṣāsana

Trikoṇāsana

Vīrabhadrāsana II

Standing Poses - continued

Parivṛtta Trikoṇāsana

Vīrabhadrāsana I

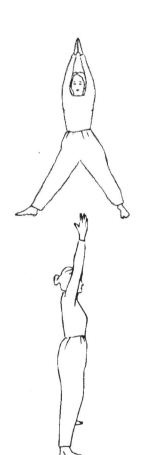

Prasārita Pādottānāsana

Hand Balances

Preparation for Handstand

 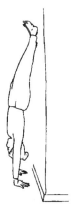 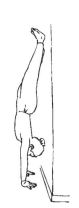

Adho Mukha Vṛkṣāsana - Handstand

Preparation for Elbow Balance

Pīncha Mayūrāsana - Elbow Balance

Hand Balances - continued

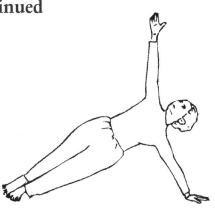

Vasiṣṭhāsana I

Dwi Hasta Bhujāsana

Bakāsana

Forward Bends

Jānu Śīrṣāsana

Upaviṣṭha Koṇāsana

Paschimottānāsana

Baddha Koṇāsana

Twists

Parivṛtta Sukhāsana - Simple Twist

Marīchyāsana III

Lying Down Twist

Backbends

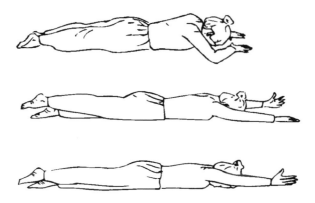

Eka Pāda Śalabhāsana:

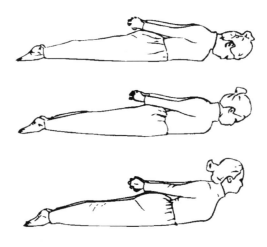

Ūrdhva Mukha Śalabhāsana:

Śalabhāsana:

Backbends - continued

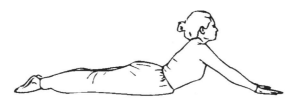

Bhujaṅgāsana

Setu Bandha

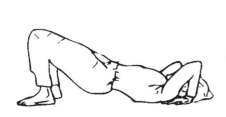  

Ūrdhva Dhanurāsana

Leg Stretches

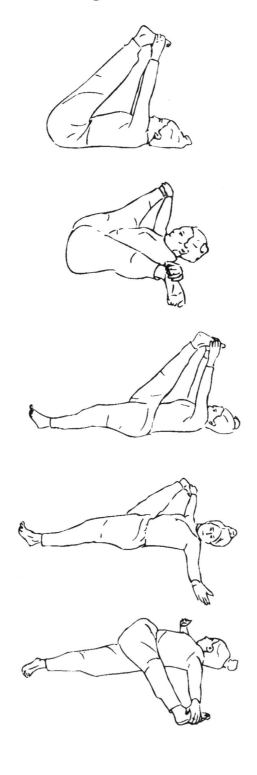

Inverted Poses

Preparation for Headstand (Śīrṣāsana)

Śīrṣāsana - Headstand

Inverted poses - continued

Halāsana - Plough

Karṇapīḍāsana

 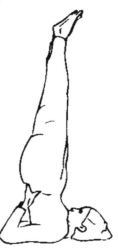

Sarvāngāsana - Shoulder Balance

Sitting Poses

Vajrāsana

Vajrāsana I   Parvatāsana   Garuḍāsana

Vīrāsana

Vīrāsana I   Parvatāsana   Gomukhāsana

Padmāsana

Ardha Padmāsana - half lotus   Padmāsana - full lotus

Śavāsana - Relaxation

Śavāsana

39096901R00020

Made in the USA
Lexington, KY
06 February 2015